Teacher's Handbook

SRA

Reading LABORATORY®

2b

McGraw Hill

SRA

mheducation.com/prek-12

Send all inquiries to:
McGraw-Hill Education
8787 Orion Place
Columbus, OH 43240

ISBN: 978-0-07-702362-1
MHID: 0-07-702362-5

Printed in the United States of America.

4 5 6 7 8 9 LHN 27 26 25 24 23

Table of Contents

Preface to the 2020 Edition

A Wealth of Good Reading

For more than sixty years, teachers have been aware of the strengths of ***SRA Reading Laboratory***—how it provides individualized skills instruction, permits independent work, promotes students' sense of responsibility, and lets each student move at his or her own rate, according to individual ability. However, there is another aspect of ***SRA Reading Laboratory*** that deserves to be stressed: the great quantity of good reading passages to be found.

The reading selections in ***SRA Reading Laboratory*** are by no means just sterile skills exercises. They are a balanced collection of fiction and nonfiction short stories and articles that students actually enjoy reading. In addition, they are sources of a great deal of incidental learning as well—about plants, animals, history, science, technology, discovery, fine arts, social institutions, sports, and different cultures.

Students don't just learn to read better by using ***SRA Reading Laboratory***; they discover what it means to become readers. They gain pleasure, information, and—if the ultimate goal succeeds—a lifelong love of reading in all kinds of subject areas. They learn to read for a variety of purposes, and they discover what it is to read in a wide range of content areas. Good reading is not just an incidental aspect of ***SRA Reading Laboratory*** but one of its principal elements and strengths.

Every new edition of ***SRA Reading Laboratory*** is updated and improved over previous editions. In this 2020 edition, many of the ***Power Builder*** selections have been replaced with brand-new selections, while other selections have been edited to bring them up to date. The nonfiction reading selections are enhanced by colorful photographs, and the fictional stories incorporate engaging illustrations to promote comprehension and reading enjoyment.

Equitable Educational Resources

The collection of readings exposes students to a balance of fiction and nonfiction genres, such as classic literature, folktales, fantasy, and informational text. In addition, the readings focus on a variety of topics, including science, technology, history, and cultures. The emphasis on student choice and engagement in ***SRA Reading Laboratory*** provides students with essential knowledge and academic vocabulary, which is just as important for a literate reader as are developing the skills of decoding, vocabulary, and structural analysis.

Virtually any interesting reading materials can be used to build skills, but materials relating to our tremendous diversity among cultures will help to build a more equitable education for all students. The ***Power Builder*** selections enable students to gain an understanding and appreciation of worldwide settings, lifestyles, problems, and perspectives.

Social and Emotional Learning

In reading the ***Power Builder*** selections, not only will students find plentiful entertainment, but they also will learn about the consequences of greed and the rewards of kindness, generosity, and honesty. They will read true stories about the accomplishments and struggles of all kinds of people throughout history.

As you use ***SRA Reading Laboratory,*** incorporate the following suggestions in your classroom to instill core social and emotional competencies in students.

- Create a continuously nurturing environment for learning but encourage individual student goal setting and progress. Reward positive behavior and help students feel ownership over their own progress.
- Integrate social and emotional skill building by giving students the opportunity for self-reflection on their own reading process.
- Communicate early and often with students and their families. Have students present their progress charts at parent-teacher conferences and discuss their progress, along with their difficulties and their successes.
- Empower students to become self-directed learners. Talk about growth mindset and make sure students understand how they can work to improve their skills. Encourage students to persist when faced with difficult tasks.

Overview: Getting to Know the Program

Goals of SRA Reading Laboratory

1 To develop comprehension, vocabulary, word analysis, and study skills

2 To reinforce specific skills to help students become proficient readers

3 To interest students in reading and to enlarge their specific knowledge, using a wide array of quality fiction and nonfiction selections

4 To develop independent readers with strong comprehension skills, endurance, and confidence

5 To develop the sense of personal responsibility as students take charge of their own learning

Methods and Goals

As a teacher, you know that students differ in how fast they learn as well as in how much they learn. A typical classroom has many levels of learning. Therefore, there is a great need for a systematic way of accommodating all those levels at the same time. ***SRA Reading Laboratory*** does precisely that.

The program meets the differing needs of students by providing multilevel learning materials in one classroom package. It is a complete system offering individualized reading opportunities to all your students. You need no additional materials or teaching assistance to operate it. In fact, it basically operates itself. After some initial training, students manage their own learning. They work independently, score their own work, and keep accurate accounts of their own progress.

The reading materials and associated skills exercises in any one ***Reading Laboratory*** are organized into a series of color-designated difficulty levels that range above and below the average for that grade or age group. The student who reads below grade level finds material that he or she can read right away. This removes the frustration of trying to read and understand material that is too difficult. At the same time, the more advanced student finds materials suited to his or her abilities. This removes the potential boredom that comes with reading materials that are too easy. Students progress according to their own abilities and at whatever pace is appropriate to each one.

You begin using the program in your classroom by giving a short six-minute test–the Starting Level Guide–to determine the color level in which each student should start. Even if your students have used the program before, it is still important to begin each school year with the Starting Level Guide and other introductory procedures in order to ensure accurate placement after periods of break time.

Students work individually and chart their progress. Once a week, you may want to have a brief individual conference with each student. By studying the progress charts with the student, you can help the student evaluate his or her work. Then you and the student can decide together whether he or she is ready to move to the next color level.

Teachers are often surprised to see how much responsibility students can take for their own learning. The more you work with multilevel teaching and learning, the more opportunities you will find for building one-to-one relationships with your students. You will also see how students' self-esteem grows with learning.

The goals of ***SRA Reading Laboratory*** go well beyond mere skills learning, although skills learning is certainly an important part of the whole. Five main goals are served by the various learning materials in ***SRA Reading Laboratory*** and by the educational method and philosophy of the multilevel system.

If you wish to review in detail the reading skills on which the program is focused, turn to the Comprehension and Word-Study Skills Charts in Appendix C of this handbook. There you can see at a glance the specific skills presented in each reading level.

See Appendix C for a listing of specific comprehension and word-study skills.

Getting the Most Out of the Program

A clear understanding of the program will help ensure that you and your students derive maximum benefit from ***SRA Reading Laboratory's*** pedagogical design. Special emphasis is given to these points at the outset so that they will not be overlooked.

1 ***SRA Reading Laboratory*** is a system that has been carefully structured for teaching and developing essential skills and beneficial attitudes in an orderly and purposeful method. When treated as a regularly scheduled part of the classroom routine, the laboratory offers you an organized, systematic program that can significantly improve reading skills, study habits, and feelings of personal responsibility.

2 ***SRA Reading Laboratory*** is a flexible program that can be easily implemented to fit into a variety of school calendars and schedules. One suggestion that has been proven effective is to use the program over a fairly concentrated period of time instead of being widely spaced across the entire school year. The recommended schedule on page 13 calls for nine practice sessions (twenty to forty minutes long) spaced closely together during the training phase and then followed by a phase in which students use the program materials independently. The program ends with a final evaluation. When practice periods are kept close together, there is carryover learning from one day to the next. When practice periods are spaced too far apart, carryover is lessened, and students tend to forget not only the information learned but even the procedures to follow.

When practice periods are kept close together, there is carryover learning from day to day.

Students will complete different numbers of ***Power Builders*** depending on their own progress.

Encourage students to take responsibility for their own learning.

3 It is not intended that every student work his or her way through *all* the ***Power Builders*** in a level or that a student work the ***Power Builders*** in strict sequence. Instead, a student selects (or is given)* ***Power Builders*** in *random* sequence from his or her assigned level; as soon as the student's scores show adequate progress (as discussed on pages 34–35), the student advances to the next color level. Thus, the number of ***Power Builders*** that any student will work in a particular level will vary according to his or her abilities and learning rate. A typical student should probably complete at least four ***Power Builders*** in a level; others may do eight or ten. Some students may require practice with all ***Power Builders*** in a level before moving on.

4 After the training phase, it is a good idea to begin holding weekly conferences with each student to review his or her progress. You are strongly encouraged to make these conferences mutual consultations in which you and the student decide together whether it is time to move to a new level. Getting students accustomed to taking responsibility for their own learning progress is important if you are to realize the full potential of ***SRA Reading Laboratory*** as not just a builder of skills but of self-image and self-confidence as well.

Although free choice of **Power Builders by individuals is consistent with the laboratory's purpose and design, you may want to implement a group-leader system to reduce the confusion resulting from traffic to and from the laboratory box. Student helpers or group leaders can hand out the Progress Charts, Record Pages, and the **Power Builders**, giving each student any **Power Builder** that he or she has not yet read in the assigned color level. In this system, the group leaders also collect the materials at the end of the period and refile the **Power Builders** in the laboratory box. Whether to use this group-leader system or to let each student select his or her materials from the box is up to you.*

Materials

SRA Reading Laboratory contains the following materials:

Teacher's Handbook

The *Teacher's Handbook* contains an overview of ***SRA Reading Laboratory*** and provides teaching plans for using the program to its maximum advantage. The separate appendixes of the References and Resources section provide detailed information about program selections, skills, and procedures.

The Student Resources section includes a Home Connection letter that should be copied and given to students to take home to provide information to parents and guardians about the program. In addition, the Student Resources section includes the Starting Level Guide, a Starter Story, Record Pages, Progress Charts, and a Percentage Conversion Table. You will copy and distribute these materials as needed.

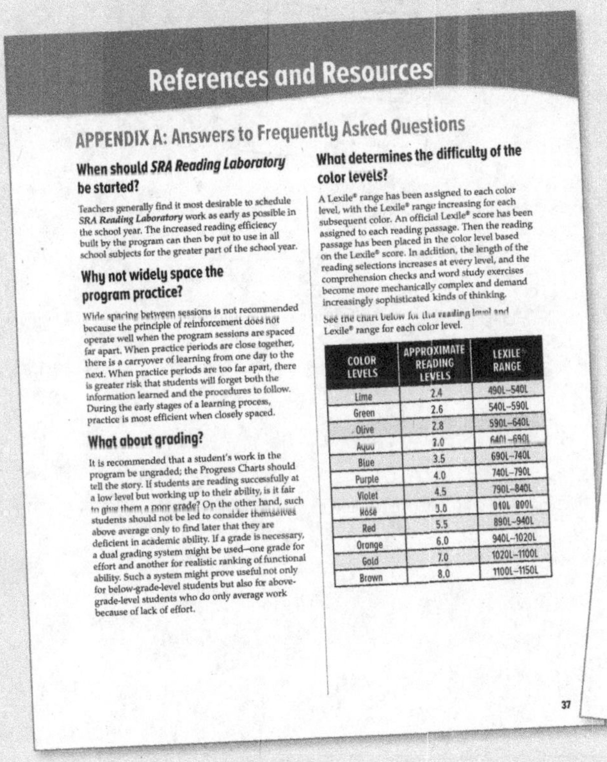
References and Resources

APPENDIX A: Answers to Frequently Asked Questions

When should *SRA Reading Laboratory* be started?

Teachers generally find it most desirable to schedule *SRA Reading Laboratory* work as early as possible in the school year. The increased reading efficiency built by the program can then be put to use in all school subjects for the greater part of the school year.

Why not widely space the program practice?

Wide spacing between sessions is not recommended because the principle of reinforcement does not operate well when the program sessions are spaced far apart. When practice periods are close together, there is a carryover of learning from one day to the next. When practice periods are too far apart, there is greater risk that students will forget both the information learned and the procedures to follow. During the early stages of a learning process, practice is most efficient when closely spaced.

What about grading?

It is recommended that a student's work in the program be ungraded; the Progress Charts should tell the story. If students are reading successfully at a low level but working up to their ability, is it fair to give them a poor grade? On the other hand, such students should not be led to consider themselves above average only to find later that they are deficient in academic ability. If a grade is necessary, a dual grading system might be used—one grade for effort and another for realistic ranking of functional ability. Such a system might prove useful not only for below-grade-level students but also for above-grade-level students who do only average work because of lack of effort.

What determines the difficulty of the color levels?

A Lexile® range has been assigned to each color level, with the Lexile® range increasing for each subsequent color. An official Lexile® score has been assigned to each reading passage. Then the reading passage has been placed in the color level based on the Lexile® score. In addition, the length of the reading selections increases at every level, and the comprehension checks and word study exercises become more mechanically complex and demand increasingly sophisticated kinds of thinking.

See the chart below for the reading level and Lexile® range for each color level.

COLOR LEVELS	APPROXIMATE READING LEVELS	LEXILE RANGE
Lime	2.4	490L–540L
Green	2.6	540L–590L
Olive	2.8	590L–640L
Aqua	3.0	640L–690L
Blue	3.5	690L–740L
Purple	4.0	740L–790L
Violet	4.5	790L–840L
Rose	[illegible]	[illegible]
Red	5.5	890L–940L
Orange	6.0	940L–1020L
Gold	7.0	1020L–1100L
Brown	8.0	1100L–1150L

37

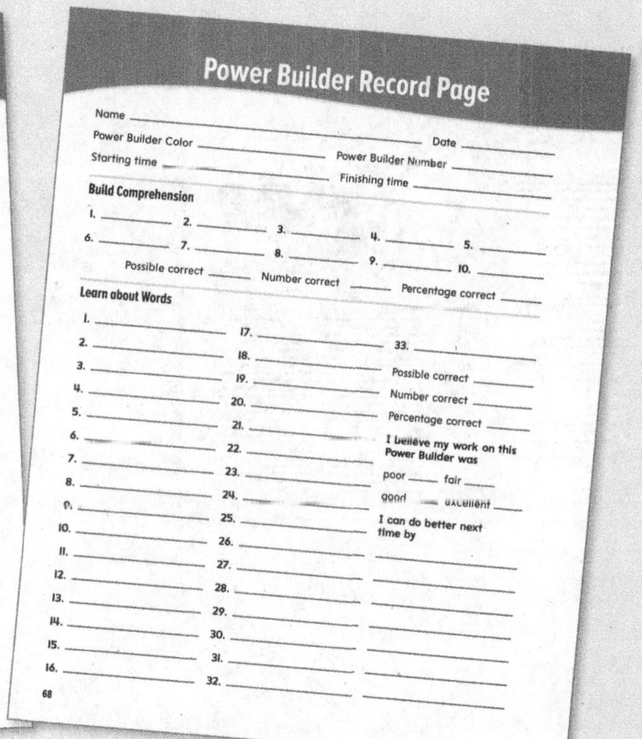
Power Builder Record Page

Name ____ Power Builder Color ____ Date ____

Starting time ____ Power Builder Number ____ Finishing time ____

Build Comprehension

1. ____ 2. ____ 3. ____ 4. ____ 5. ____
6. ____ 7. ____ 8. ____ 9. ____ 10. ____

Possible correct ____ Number correct ____ Percentage correct ____

Learn about Words

1. ____ through 16. ____; 17. ____ through 32. ____; 33. ____

Possible correct ____
Number correct ____
Percentage correct ____

I believe my work on this Power Builder was
poor ____ fair ____
good ____ excellent ____

I can do better next time by

68

Materials

Power Builders

This is the core component of *SRA Reading Laboratory.* The 144 four-page *Power Builders* are arranged in color-coded levels of graduated difficulty. Each *Power Builder* has three parts:

1. High-interest fiction or nonfiction reading selection that includes engaging illustrations or photographs
2. Build Comprehension section that contains multileveled questions about the reading selection
3. Learn about Words section that includes exercises on vocabulary and word-study skills

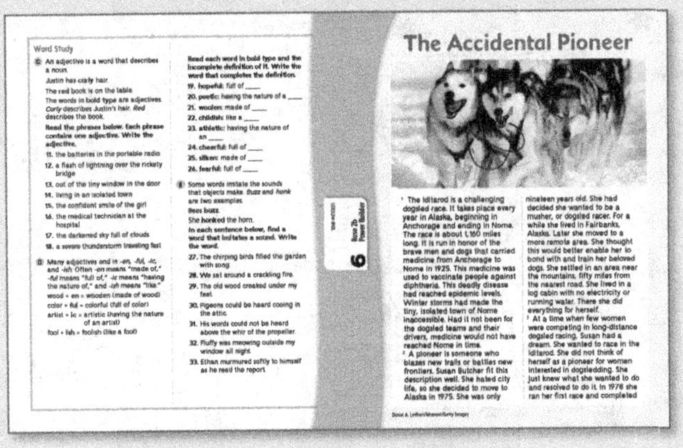

Power Builder Key Cards

Every *Power Builder* has a corresponding *Key Card* with the answers to the *Power Builder* questions. Students use the *Key Card* to score their own work.

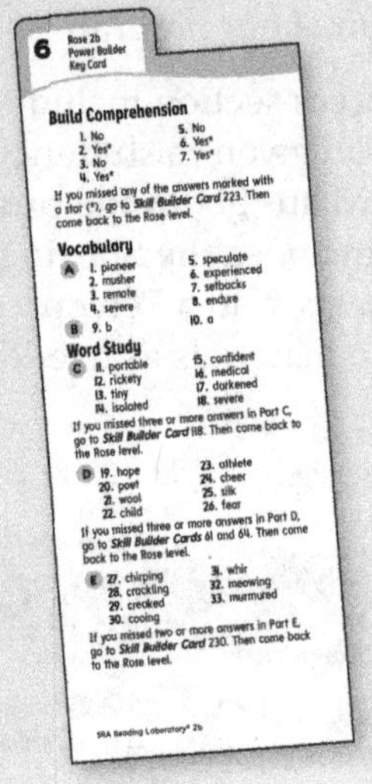

Skill Builders

These lessons provide reinforcement in basic comprehension, phonics, grammar, and word-study skills.

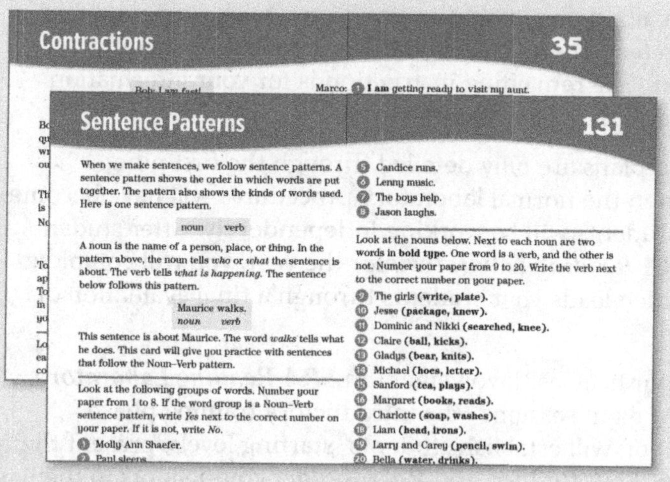

Skill Builder Key Cards

These *Key Cards* enable students to score their work from *Skill Builders*.

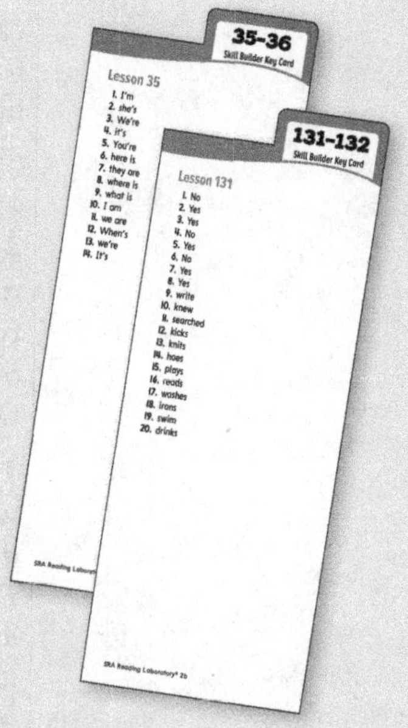

Rate Builders

These are 144 very short, timed reading selections designed to help students read faster while maintaining comprehension. Students are given exactly three minutes to read a selection and answer the questions that follow it. Like the *Power Builders*, the *Rate Builders* are organized into color levels of graduated difficulty.

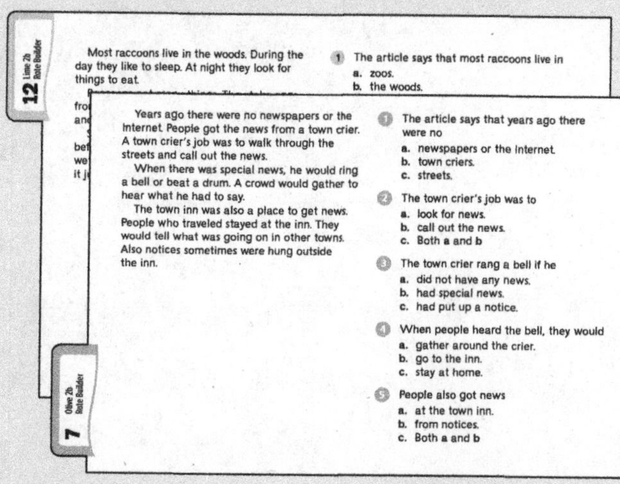

Rate Builder Key Cards

Students can check their work in *Rate Builders* using these *Key Cards.*

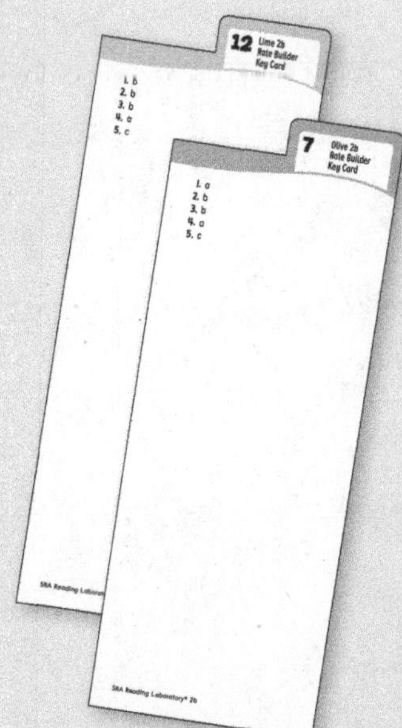

Recommended Schedule and Teaching Plans

The following schedule covers a training phase and an independent phase for using the program materials. It is considered best to schedule the ***Power Builder*** sessions close together. Each day's session is assumed to be twenty to forty minutes long.

To facilitate instruction, the teaching plans are "scripted" so that you can read them aloud directly to the class if you wish (or paraphrase them if you prefer). These instructions are signaled by shading behind the text. The remaining instruction is for your information and is not meant to be read aloud.

These teaching plans are fully detailed through the first nine sessions. By then the normal laboratory procedures will have become routine, and students will be working independently. After students finish with ***SRA Reading Laboratory*** for the year, you will complete Session 10, which leads your students through a final evaluation of the program.

The time of your heaviest involvement in ***SRA Reading Laboratory*** will be the first eight sessions–the introductory training phase during which you will establish students' starting levels, present the ***Power Builder***, ***Skill Builder***, and ***Rate Builder*** components to them, and give them opportunities to practice the basic procedures.

During the remainder of the program, students will be working independently for the most part. Your role will be primarily that of a manager/consultant who sets the times for ***SRA Reading Laboratory*** sessions and holds conferences with individual students to review their progress and help them decide whether they are ready to move to a new level.

Recommended Teaching Schedule

Training Phase

SESSION 1	SESSION 2	SESSION 3	SESSION 4	SESSION 5
Student Placement: Starting Level Guide *Page 14*	Reading Laboratory Introduction *Page 18*	Power Builder Starter *Page 20*	Power Builder Conversion Table and Progress Chart *Page 23*	Power Builders: Independent Use *Page 25*
SESSION 6	**SESSION 7**	**SESSION 8**	**SESSION 9**	**SESSION 10**
Power Builders: Comprehension and SQR Formula *Page 29*	Power Builders: Learn about Words *Page 31*	Skill Builders; Rate Builders *Page 32*	Student Conferences *Page 34*	Final Evaluation *Page 36*

Independent Phase

Follow up with more *Power Builder* sessions, spaced closely together, and end the program with a final analysis or evaluation. (See page 36.)

Student Placement: Starting Level Guide

SESSION 1

Summary: Today you will administer the Starting Level Guide, found in the Student Resources section at the back of this Handbook. It is the device for determining the color level at which each student should enter the ***Power Builder*** component. The Starting Level Guide also gives students a first taste of what it is like to read a ***Power Builder*** story and answer the associated questions.

Procedures

Take a look at the Starting Level Guide on pages 60–63 before class. It begins with six questions, followed by three stories (one of which is an example). When you administer the Starting Level Guide, make sure you allow enough time for students to complete all three stories during the same class session; otherwise, the results will not be accurate.

Make copies of the Starting Level Guide on pages 60–63 for each student. Staple the pages and distribute a packet to each student.

Read aloud or paraphrase the instructions in the shaded boxes.

SOME of you have worked with ***SRA Reading Laboratory*** before. If so, these procedures will be familiar to you.

Today we will find the best place for each of you to start building better reading skills. How do we do this? We use something called a Starting Level Guide. Let's look at the first page together.

At the top of the page, write your name and the date.

Next, go over the six questions one at a time to make sure students understand them. Then, have students answer the questions in the spaces provided. Do not let them discuss their responses with each other.

LOOK at the bottom part of the page. Below the six questions are directions and a short paragraph. Read the directions silently while I read them aloud.

Read the directions and let students ask questions.

REMEMBER to circle the letter of your answer. For example, the answer to Question 1 of the example story is *a, b, c,* or *d.* Choose the letter you think is correct, and circle it. If you want to change your answer, make an X through the circle, and circle your new answer.

Now read the example story, and answer both of the questions.

Allow about one minute for everyone to finish.

STOP! Put your pencils down. Now we will see how well you understood what you just read.

Read aloud the first comprehension question. Then call on a student to give his or her response to it. Ask the student to say not only the letter, but also the words that go with it: for example, *b, eighteen feet.* Before giving the correct response, ask whether other students have different answers. If so, guide them to reread that part of the paragraph where the correct answer can be found. Confirm that *b* is the correct answer and proceed in the same way with the second comprehension question, to which the correct answer is *c, a house cat.*

NEXT, you will read two more stories followed by questions. These stories will be a little longer and will be followed by more questions. When I give the signal, you will look at the second page and find Story A.

Then you will have three minutes to read the entire story at the top of the page and to read and answer the five questions under it. You may look back at the story. Read as rapidly as you can without losing the meaning of what you are reading. When you've answered all the questions, stop. Ready? Look at the second page. Start reading.

Look at your watch immediately. Exact timing is very important on Stories A and B. Give students three minutes to finish their work.

STOP working. Now we are going to do the other story, Story B. When I give the signal, you will turn the page to Story B. This story is a little longer, and it has eight questions. Some of you may not finish reading it and answering all the questions before I call time, but that's all right. Just do as much as you can. Read rapidly but not so fast that you miss the meaning. When you come to the bottom of the page, turn to the next page where there are three more questions. Ready? Begin reading Story B.

Give students three minutes to finish their work.

STOP working.

Collect the packet from each student. To check the Starting Level Guides, use the following key. Each student's score is the sum of his or her correct answers to Story A and Story B. Use the following placement chart to determine each student's starting level for the *Power Builder* component.

Answer Key for Starting Level Guide

Story A	Story B
1. b	1. c
2. a	2. d
3. c	3. a
4. a	4. d
5. b	5. c
	6. b
	7. b
	8. d

2b Placement Chart

Student's Score	Suggested Starting Placement
3 or below	Lime
4	Lime
5	Olive
6	Aqua
7	Purple
8	Purple
9	Violet
10 or above	Rose

Find the student's score in the left column. Start the student in the corresponding color level from the right column.

The color levels on the chart correspond to the Lexile® ranges and approximate reading levels as follows:

Color	Lexile® Range	Reading Level
Lime	490L–540L	2.4
Olive	590L–640L	2.8
Aqua	640L–690L	3.0
Purple	740L–790L	4.0
Violet	790L–840L	4.5
Rose	840L–890L	5.0

Store the student's Starting Level Guides for reference during the Final Analysis session.

Reading Laboratory Introduction

SESSION 2

Summary: Today you will introduce the concept of this multilevel learning program and acquaint students with the various components.

Procedures

Talk with students about the result of the Starting Level Guides they completed. Explain that there are various reading levels in the class. Then, present the components of the ***SRA Reading Laboratory*** to them. Begin by holding up a ***Power Builder***.

THERE are 144 of these ***Power Builders.*** Each one begins with an interesting story, followed by some questions. These ***Power Builders*** are separated into groups by color. One of these colors will be just right for you as your start out. When you have material that is just right for you, you can read more easily and understand what you read. I'll tell each of you which color you should start with, based on the results of the Starting Level Guide. That color level is where you'll begin the program. In time, as you improve your skills, you will move to other colors.

Make a copy of the Power Builder Record Page from page 68 and hold it up.

THIS is a Power Builder Record Page. You will write all your answers to the ***Power Builder*** questions on a Record Page. You must never write on a ***Power Builder*** because other students will use it after you.

Hold up a ***Power Builder Key Card.***

THIS is a ***Power Builder Key Card***. It has the answers to the questions on the matching ***Power Builder.*** Each ***Power Builder*** has its own ***Key Card***. If you find you've made a mistake, you should always look back at the ***Power Builder*** to see where you have misunderstood. For certain errors, you will be told to go to a ***Skill Builder*** lesson to help you with skills in which you need to practice.

Hold up a ***Skill Builder,*** a ***Skill Builder Key Card,*** and a copy of the Skill Builder Record Page from page 72 from this handbook.

THIS is a ***Skill Builder.*** It also has questions for you to answer. But instead of using a Power Builder Record Page to write your answers, you will write them on a plain piece of paper. Then you will check the answers with a ***Skill Builder Key Card*** and record your scores on a Skill Builder Record page.

Hold up a ***Rate Builder,*** a ***Rate Builder Key Card,*** and a copy of the Rate Builder Record Page from page 70.

THIS is a ***Rate Builder,*** which will help you improve your reading rate, or speed. The ***Rate Builders*** have the same colors as the ***Power Builders.*** When you begin, your ***Rate Builder*** color will be the same as your ***Power Builder*** color. You will use the ***Rate Builder Key Card*** to check your answers to the questions. And you will write your answers on a Rate Builder Record Page.

Power Builder Procedures

SESSION 3

Summary: Today you will work with students so they can learn the *Power Builder* procedures. You and your students will work through the Power Builder Starter together.

Procedures

Before the session, make copies of the Power Builder Starter on pages 64–67, the Power Builder Record Page on page 68, and the Power Builder Starter Key on page 74. Distribute the copies to each student.

ORDINARILY you will read the ***Power Builder*** stories to yourselves, but today I'm going to read a sample story to you. Look at the story. It's just like the ***Power Builders*** I showed you from the laboratory box. As I read, look at the story and read along silently.

TIP: For organization, have students record their answers in a notebook or have a designated folder for each student to keep track of his or her Record Pages and Progress Charts.

When you have finished reading, instruct students to write their names and the date in the spaces at the top of the Record Page.

REMEMBER that you will always write your answers on pages like this one. Never write on a ***Power Builder.***

The next space is for the ***Power Builder*** color. There you will write the name of the color level in which you are working. After that there is a space for you to write the number that is on your ***Power Builder.*** Since we are working on the Starter story, skip the color space and write *S* next to Power Builder number. Put your finger where it says Build Comprehension. This is where you will write the answers to the questions for the Starter story. Let's look at those questions now.

Read aloud the directions for the Build Comprehension section. Then read Question 1. Ask a student to give a response. If other students do not agree, invite them to look back at the story and read the part that supports the answer they chose. Tell students that looking back is always permitted, as it can help them think through a question. Then ask them to return to the Record Page and write the correct letter *(c)* after Number 1.

Remind students that when they record their answers, they should never make erasures. To change an answer, they should simply draw an X through the answer and write their new answer alongside.

When you are sure everyone knows how to proceed, let each student read silently and respond to the remaining five comprehension questions. When they have finished, write the correct responses on the board (1: c, 2: a, 3: c, 4: b, 5: a, 6: c).

IF your answers are the same as these, leave them just as they are. If you have a different answer, it is incorrect. To show that it is incorrect, draw a circle around it and write the correct letter beside it.

Remind students that it is okay to get answers wrong. The questions are not for a grade, but for accurate placement to increase learning.

Ask the class to find the Learn about Words section. Read aloud the introduction and instructions in Section A. Have students turn back to the paragraph referenced in the first question (paragraph 2) and find the word that best fits the meaning "very big." Have them write the correct answer *(gigantic)* on the Record Page. Then let each student read silently and respond to the remaining six items in Section A. Allow enough time for a majority of the students to complete the work.

Write the correct answers for Section A on the board. Have students correct their work as before. Then let them finish the remaining thirty-three items in Learn about Words.

The correct answers for Section A are:
1. gigantic
2. bushy
3. culprit
4. signs
5. bulge
6. rotate
7. drifted

Ask the class to use the Power Builder Starter Key to check their answers to the questions in Sections B, C, D, and E.

Make sure students take time to learn from their mistakes. Whenever they make a mistake, they should refer back to the ***Power Builder*** selection, see why they responded as they did, and reflect on why another response is better. This immediate-feedback procedure is far more beneficial than merely accepting the verdict on the ***Key Card*** and moving on. Comprehension skills will be strengthened if students perform this review for every mistake.

When all students have finished, ask them to look at the lower half of the right-hand column of the Record Page, evaluate their work, and decide how they could do better next time.

THAT is all we're going to do today. Tomorrow you will learn how to score your work and mark a Power Builder Progress Chart.

Collect the Power Builder Starter story and the Record Page from each student. Do not be discouraged if not all students complete the work in their first ***Power Builder*** experience. Later you will have time to help slower students master the procedures. If a number of students have difficulty with this session, you can form a small group apart from the rest of the class and review the Power Builder Starter with them after this session.

Power Builder: Conversion Table and Progress Chart

Summary: Today you will show students the procedures for using a Progress Chart to keep an accurate record of their work. This entails using the Conversion Table to determine the percentage score and posting this information in the Power Builder Progress Chart.

SESSION 4

Procedures

Make copies of the Power Builder Progress Chart on page 69 and the Conversion Table on page 73 for each student. Distribute the copies along with each student's completed Record Page from the previous day.

> **YESTERDAY** you learned how to read a *Power Builder* and complete the exercises. You also learned to record your answers on a Record Page.

Look at the Build Comprehension section on your Record Page. Notice that there are ten blanks in that section. Some *Power Builders* have as many as ten comprehension questions; others have only five. For the *Power Builder* that we read yesterday, there were 6 questions, so write *6* on the line next to "Possible correct" on your Record Page.

Now, look at your circled letters on your Record Page. These indicate your incorrect answers. Of the six possible correct answers, determine how many you got correct and write that number on the line next to "Number correct" on your Record Page.

Now, look at the blank after "Percentage correct." We will discuss how to determine that number next.

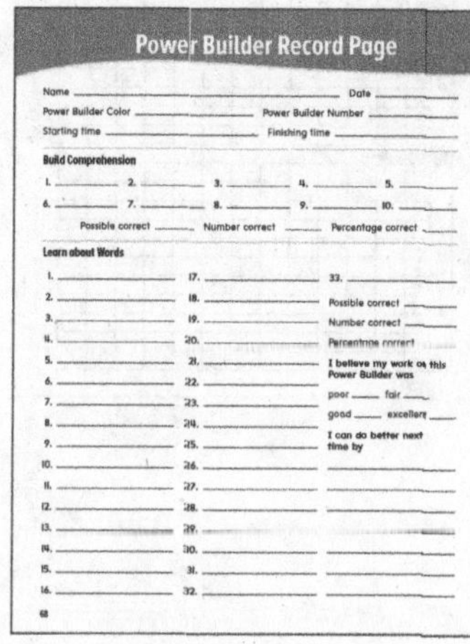

Power Builder Record Page

Name ______ Date ______
Power Builder Color ______ Power Builder Number ______
Starting time ______ Finishing time ______

Build Comprehension

1. ____ 2. ____ 3. ____ 4. ____ 5. ____
6. ____ 7. ____ 8. ____ 9. ____ 10. ____

Possible correct ____ Number correct ____ Percentage correct ____

Learn about Words

1. ____ 17. ____ 33. ____
2. ____ 18. ____ Possible correct ____
3. ____ 19. ____ Number correct ____
4. ____ 20. ____ Percentage correct ____
5. ____ 21. ____ I believe my work on this Power Builder was
6. ____ 22. ____ poor ____ fair ____
7. ____ 23. ____ good ____ excellent ____
8. ____ 24. ____ I can do better next time by
9. ____ 25. ____
10. ____ 26. ____
11. ____ 27. ____
12. ____ 28. ____
13. ____ 29. ____
14. ____ 30. ____
15. ____ 31. ____
16. ____ 32. ____

68

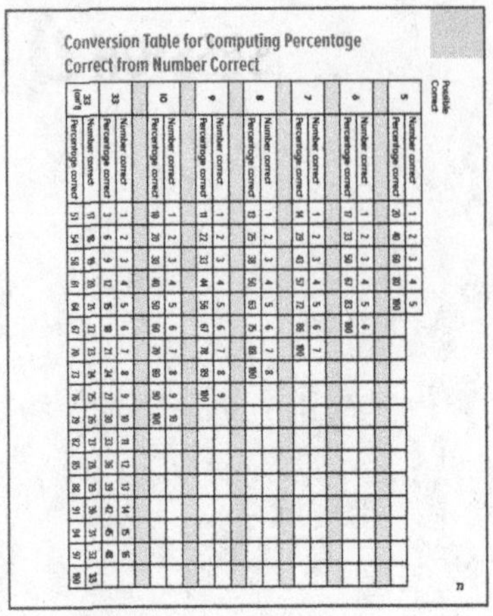
Conversion Table for Computing Percentage Correct from Number Correct

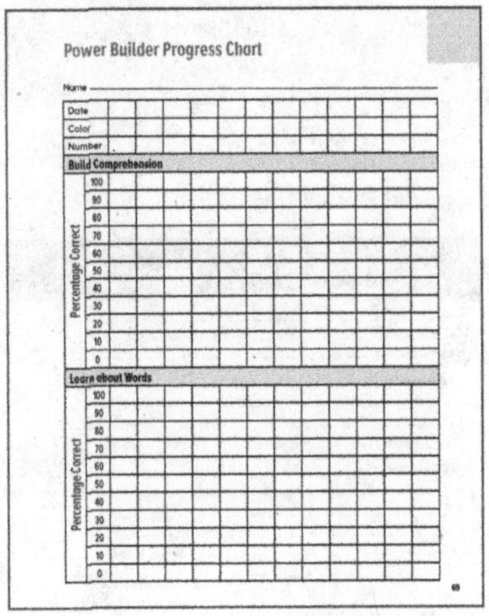
Power Builder Progress Chart

LOOK at the Conversion Table and look at the left column under "Possible Correct." Since there were 6 questions, look at the table next to "6". Look in the "Number correct" row and find your number of correct answers. Then find the percentage correct for that number. Enter the percentage on your Record Page.

Have students follow the same procedures for the Learn about Words section, entering 33 after "Possible correct" and his or her score after "Number correct." Then have students determine their percentage using the Conversion Table and enter the percentage on their Record Page.

Now, have students look at the Progress Chart. Tell them to enter their names at the top of the chart. Then have students enter the date at the top of the first column. In the first space following the word *Number*, have them write *S* for *Starter*. Tell students to leave the space blank after the word *Color*.

LOOK at the section next to Build Comprehension. Use your pencil to make a line in the box where your percentage correct falls. If it does not fall on an even number such as 70 or 80, use your eye to estimate where you should draw the line.

Follow these same steps for Learn about Words to show your percentage correct for that section.

Now fill in the column from each zero baseline up to each of your lines.

While students are doing this, walk around the class and look at the charts. Offer help as needed. When everyone has finished, collect each student's Progress Chart.

Power Builders: Independent Use

Summary: Today students will begin working with *Power Builders* independently at their own level. First, however, you may want to review the *Power Builder* procedures with students.

In general allow approximately a thirty to forty-five minute period of time for students to work each *Power Builder.* Due to individual differences, students will work at different speeds. Early in the program, some students may require more time to complete a *Power Builder.* Later in the program, some students will finish their work early. However, these students should not begin another *Power Builder.* If work is hurried, a student's work may degenerate into a pointless race with time. If students have time remaining, allow them to do an activity that is a change of pace. For example, you could allow them to read library books or other materials for pleasure.

Procedures

Before the session begins, you will need to decide the general procedure for using *Power Builders* in your classroom. You can either have students select their own *Power Builders* individually, or you may want to appoint group leaders in charge of selecting the *Power Builders* and handing them out.*

Next, choose a *Power Builder* for each student based on his or her assigned color level. Make copies of the Power Builder Record Page and retrieve each student's Power Builder Progress Chart. Distribute the chosen *Power Builder,* the Progress Chart, and a copy of the Record Page to each student.

YOU have been learning how to work with *Power Builders,* using the Starter story. Now you will begin to work with the actual *Power Builders.*

**You should establish goals that work for your class. Individual student choice encourages personal responsibility. Assigning group leaders and rotating leadership roles fosters a team approach and encourages leadership skills.*

SESSION 5

Encourage students to take responsibility and pride in their independent work and progress.

THIS is the color in which you will start your *Power Builder* work. It is the color that was indicated by the Starting Level Guide you took a few days ago. Look at the color and the number showing on your *Power Builder.* It is on the edge of your *Power Builder.*

Look at the number of your *Power Builder.* Now look on your Progress Chart. In the second column, write today's date, and the color and number of your *Power Builder.* You will do this each time you receive a new *Power Builder.* In this way your chart will always show which *Power Builders* you have already completed, so you won't repeat the same one twice.

You can read the *Power Builders* within your color in any order. For example, you could read Number 12 first and Number 1 last. You will need to work on *Power Builders* within the same color until your scores show that you are ready to move to another level. Most of the time, you will need to complete at least four *Power Builders* before going on to the next level. You may also need to do some Skill Builder lessons as indicated on the *Power Builder Key Card.* Remember, your work is not a race. Work at the right pace for you to improve your reading skills. This will be different for everyone.

You might want to have a conference with your students after they complete four stories to see if they are ready to move to the next level.

Have students look at the Record Page.

BEFORE you read the ***Power Builder,*** write the date and the color and number of the ***Power Builder*** on a Record Page.

Look down the column to where it says "Starting time" and "Finishing time." Before you begin, look at the clock and record your starting time. After you finish reading the story and completing the questions, look at the clock again and record your finishing time.

Hold up a ***Power Builder*** and a matching ***Key Card*** from the ***Reading Laboratory*** box.

REMEMBER, each ***Power Builder*** has its own ***Power Builder Key Card.*** When you finish your ***Power Builder,*** go to the ***Reading Laboratory*** box, and get the matching ***Key Card.*** Using your Record Page and the ***Key Card,*** check your answers. On your Record Page, circle any incorrect answers, and write the correct answer next to each incorrect answer.

As you learned yesterday, you will fill in the "Possible correct" and "Number correct" spaces. Then you will use the Conversion Table to find your percentage and fill in the "Percentage correct" space. Finally, you will complete your Progress Chart by drawing a line in the appropriate percentage space and then filling in the column from each zero baseline up to each of your lines. This is an important step in tracking your progress in your reading journey.

Encourage students to use their Progress Charts during parent-teacher meetings. Students can explain to their parents or guardians what the Progress Chart demonstrates. This will encourage students to take ownership over their own learning.

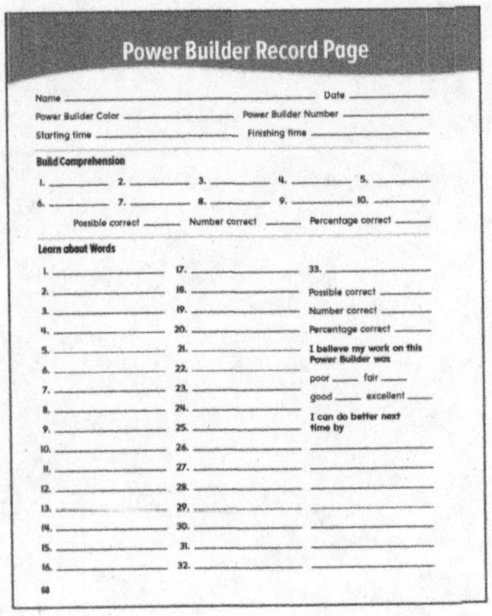

Power Builder Record Page

Name ______ Date ______
Power Builder Color ______ Power Builder Number ______
Starting time ______ Finishing time ______

Build Comprehension

1. ___ 2. ___ 3. ___ 4. ___ 5. ___
6. ___ 7. ___ 8. ___ 9. ___ 10. ___

Possible correct ___ Number correct ___ Percentage correct ___

Learn about Words

1.–32. ______
33. ______
Possible correct ______
Number correct ______
Percentage correct ______
I believe my work on this Power Builder was
poor ___ fair ___
good ___ excellent ___
I can do better next time by

68

THE last step is to evaluate your work. Look in the right column on the Record Page. This is where you will rate your work as poor, fair, good, or excellent. Then you should write two or three sentences telling how you can do better with the next ***Power Builder.***

Now that you know every step of the ***Power Builder*** process, you are ready to start working with the ***Power Builder*** on your own. Ask me at any time if you are not sure what to do next.

Power Builders: Comprehension and SQR Formula

SESSION 6

Summary: Today you will provide some useful hints about answering comprehension questions, and you will discuss the SQR (Survey, Question, Read) technique with students prior to having them work on a ***Power Builder*** on their own.

Procedures

THE comprehension checks ("Build Comprehension") that follow the ***Power Builder*** selections will help you increase your reading and thinking skills. There are three things to watch for when doing comprehension checks.

First—Pay special attention to the words that begin each question. They will give you very useful clues. They will tell you what kinds of reading and thinking skills you will need to use. For example: "The main idea of this story is" tells you to think about the story as a whole, not about small, unimportant facts.

Second—Don't jump to conclusions. Read ***all*** the possible responses and then choose the best answer. Be especially careful when one of the possible responses is "Both **a** and **b**" or "Neither **a** nor **b**."

Third—Watch out for words like ***always, never, all,*** and ***none***. A statement may be true sometimes, but not always.

Remind students that sometimes they will need to read a comprehension question more than once to understand it fully. Also, reinforce the importance of reading through the question and the answer choices completely before choosing the correct answer.

Before students begin working with their ***Power Builders,*** conduct a brief discussion of the SQR (Survey, Question, Read) technique.

Hold up a ***Power Builder*** and show students the front cover and the story. Tell them to look at the art on the front cover. On the board, write the word *Survey,* using an oversized *S*. Explain that this word means "to look over" and that they have just been surveying the ***Power Builder.***

Ask students if any questions occurred to them as they surveyed. When some students have responded, write the word *Question* (oversized *Q*) under the word *Survey*. Under the word *Question,* write the word *Read* (oversized *R*).

HERE you have a formula that will help you read and study better–SQR. First you Survey, then you Question, and then you are ready to Read–and to understand what you read. You will practice using this formula with the ***Power Builders.***

Allow students to work independently on their ***Power Builders.***

Power Builders: Learn about Words

SESSION 7

Summary: Today, you will go over the Learn about Words section before having students work another *Power Builder.* Continue during this session and in those sessions that follow to give students individual help—procedural and otherwise—whenever they need it.

Procedures

Distribute a ***Power Builder*** to each student. Ask the class to turn to the Learn about Words section. Discuss the main sections—Vocabulary and Word Study. Point out that Part A presents words in context. Remind students that they can often tell the meaning of a word by reading the words around it. Part B is a vocabulary activity that refers students to words used within the selection. Parts C through E present a variety of word-meaning and word-building activities.

Let students work on their ***Power Builders.*** Remind them to use the SQR technique, and to ask for help whenever they need it.

Skill Builders; Rate Builders

SESSION 8

Summary: In this session, you will make sure students understand the purpose and use of the *Skill Builders* and the *Rate Builders.* Students need to understand the purpose and use of these components in reinforcing specific skills in comprehension, vocabulary, word study, grammar, and fluency.

Procedures

Hold up a ***Power Builder Key Card.*** Point out the words that direct students to the numbered ***Skill Builders.*** Make sure they understand that they must first complete the scoring of their work with the ***Power Builder Key Card*** and then obtain and work the ***Skill Builder*** to which they have been referred.

> **LET'S** pretend this is a ***Key Card*** for a ***Power Builder*** I have just done, and that I have missed some questions. The ***Key Card*** tells me to go to one or more of the ***Skill Builders.*** On some days, I may not miss any of the important questions, so I won't need to go to these additional lessons. However, on this day, I have missed some. So after checking all my answers with the ***Key Card,*** I return the ***Key Card*** to the box and take out the ***Skill Builder*** to which I've been sent. Let's say it's Lesson 10.

Hold up the Lesson 10 ***Skill Builder*** and ***Skill Builder Key Card.***

> **I** will read the lesson and work the exercises. I will write my answers on a piece of paper. Of course, I never write on the ***Skill Builder.*** Then I will check my work with a ***Key Card,*** just as I did with my ***Power Builder.*** The ***Skill Builders*** have their own ***Key Cards,*** which are found here in the box. I will use the ***Key Card*** to check my work, and then record my score on a Record Page.

Show students the ***Skill Builder*** Record Page from page 72. Point out that there is no Progress Chart for ***Skill Builders.***

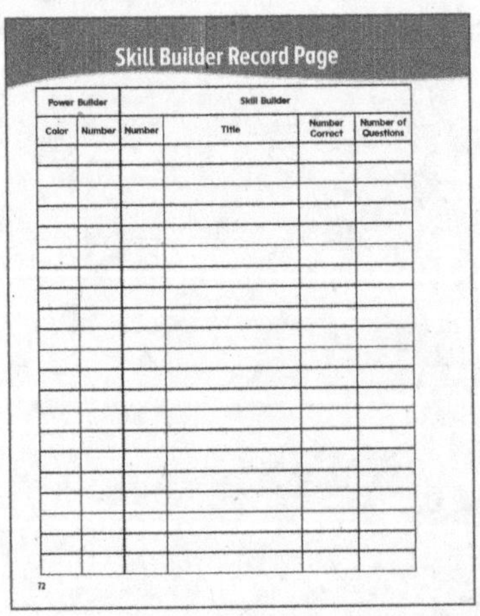
Skill Builder Record Page

Power Builder		Skill Builder			
Color	Number	Number	Title	Number Correct	Number of Questions

72

Hold up a ***Rate Builder*** and ***Rate Builder Key Card.***

THIS is a ***Rate Builder.*** It will help you improve your reading rate, or speed. The ***Rate Builders*** have the same colors as the ***Power Builders.*** When you begin, your ***Rate Builder*** color will be the same as your ***Power Builder*** color. You will move from level to level just as you do in the ***Power Builders.*** However, in time you may move into ***Rate Builders*** that are a different color from your ***Power Builder*** level.

Part of the fun of doing ***Rate Builders*** is that they take only three minutes. In the ***Power Builders,*** each of you will work at your own speed. However, we will do the ***Rate Builders*** as a class. ***Rate Builders*** are to be completed in three minutes, and I will keep track of the time. You'll have exactly three minutes to read the selection, read the questions, and write your answers on a ***Rate Builder*** Record page. You will record your ***Rate Builder*** scores and then chart your score on a Progress Chart just as you do with the ***Power Builders.***

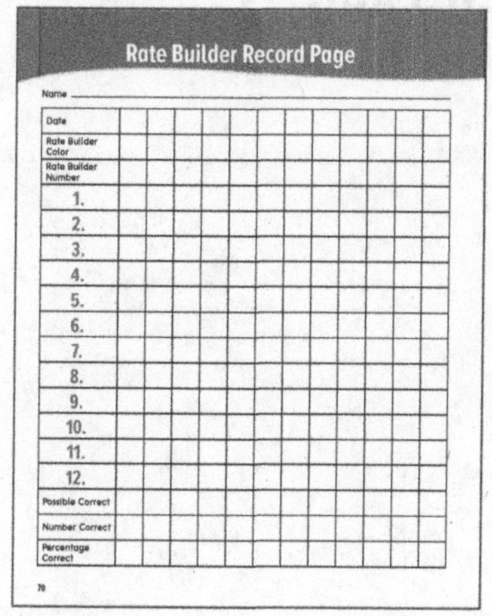
Rate Builder Record Page

Name

Date
Rate Builder Color
Rate Builder Number
1.
2.
3.
4.
5.
6.
7.
8.
9.
10.
11.
12.
Possible Correct
Number Correct
Percentage Correct

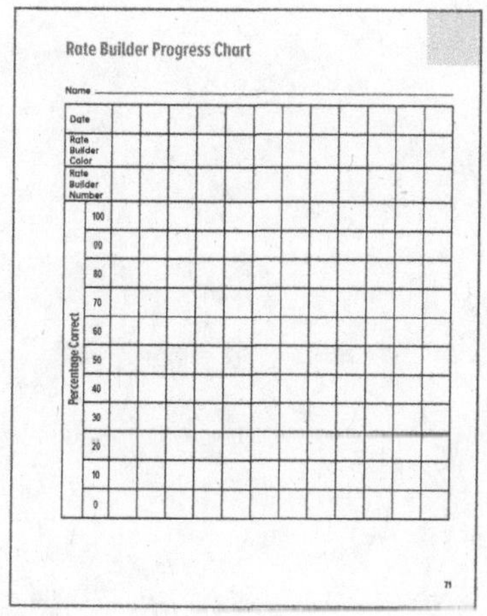
Rate Builder Progress Chart

Name

Date
Rate Builder Color
Rate Builder Number
Percentage Correct
100
90
80
70
60
50
40
30
20
10
0

Student Conferences

SESSION 9

Summary: Today you'll review the work individual students have been doing. One of the first things you want to find out is whether each student has been placed in the correct color and corresponding Lexile® level. The Starting Level Guide you administered earlier is not a precise instrument, although it is a good general indicator of the best level at which a student should begin. Psychological factors, some uneasiness about working under pressure of time, or simply lucky guessing may result in better or worse performance with the Starting Level Guide than actual ability warrants. If this is the case, it should become apparent now as you review each student's Progress Chart, and an adjustment of the student's placement can be made.

Procedures

Once the ***Power Builder*** procedures are established, you will hold a counseling session with each student. While the class is working with ***Power Builders*** or doing free reading, begin conferencing with individual students. Ask a student to come to your desk, bringing along his or her Progress Chart. Begin by asking the student how he or she is doing and how he or she is enjoying the work. Then examine the Progress Chart. If you have any questions about how accurately the chart reflects the student's true abilities, he or she should read to you from one of the ***Power Builders*** so you can make a more direct assessment.

To the greatest extent possible, your student conferences should be cooperative ventures in which you and the student reach a decision together regarding the student's performance. The student should be encouraged to help decide whether he or she is ready to advance to a new level, or whether remaining in the current level for a while longer is appropriate. Students unused to having such responsibility for their own instruction and progress will probably be a little hesitant to join in the decision at first. Soon, however, they will become accustomed to the idea and will acquire considerable skill in analyzing their work.

In these conferences, students may reveal certain concerns. They may feel ashamed to make mistakes. If so, explain that it is natural to make mistakes and that mistakes can help you learn, provided you take the time to find out why you made the mistake.

Students may be worried because of the irregular appearance—highs and lows—of their Progress Charts. Explain that there is no perfect progress from day to day. The important thing is the general direction in which they are moving.

Students may be worried about competition with others. Emphasize that students develop at different rates. The important thing is each student's development. Students who advance through the lower levels make as much progress as those who advance through the higher levels.

Individual development and progress is the goal.

Advancing to a Higher Color Level

It is during these student conferences that you will consider whether students are ready to move to a higher color level. During the program, some students can be expected to advance three, four, or even five color levels.

Generally, a typical student should complete four to six ***Power Builders*** and achieve scores of 85 to 100 percent in both the Comprehension and the Learn about Words sections before moving to a higher color level. Some students may need to finish all the ***Power Builders*** before moving to a new color level.

Occasionally, students will not want to advance because they enjoy the success they are having with the easier work. Then you will have to prod them a little. On the other hand, there are always a few students who are too anxious to advance. You will tactfully have to slow their progress without destroying their enthusiasm. In either case, the Progress Charts are the basis for wise decisions.

Use the Progress Charts to help you differentiate instruction if needed.

Final Evaluation

SESSION 10

Summary: When your class has finished ***Power Builders*** for the year, lead a class discussion of what they have learned about reading and what they have enjoyed about ***SRA Reading Laboratory.*** Careful attention to students' comments can help you identify ways to work more effectively with individuals and the class as a whole.

Procedures

Distribute each student's Starting Level Guide and ask them to look at the first page. Call students' attention to the first part of the Starting Level Guide—the beginning inventory, where they recorded their reading habits, out-of-school activities, and so on.

> **ON** the first day of using *SRA Reading Laboratory,* you answered some questions in the Starting Level Guide. Now that you have worked with the multilevel program, let's read those questions again.

Allow a few minutes for students to read. Then ask them to look at the Final Evaluation section on the last page of the Starting Level Guide. Allow a few minutes for students to read the six questions. Then ask them to write their answers to the questions, answering each one honestly and completely.

When students have finished writing, collect the Starting Level Guide from each student. Compare each individual's impressions and hopes at the beginning of the program with his or her evaluations and suggestions at the end. This analysis can show you how to work more effectively to help your students.

APPENDIX A: Answers to Frequently Asked Questions

When should *SRA Reading Laboratory* be started?

Teachers generally find it most desirable to schedule *SRA Reading Laboratory* work as early as possible in the school year. The increased reading efficiency built by the program can then be put to use in all school subjects for the greater part of the school year.

Why not widely space the program practice?

Wide spacing between sessions is not recommended because the principle of reinforcement does not operate well when the program sessions are spaced far apart. When practice periods are close together, there is a carryover of learning from one day to the next. When practice periods are too far apart, there is greater risk that students will forget both the information learned and the procedures to follow. During the early stages of a learning process, practice is most efficient when closely spaced.

What about grading?

It is recommended that a student's work in the program be ungraded; the Progress Charts should tell the story. If students are reading successfully at a low level but working up to their ability, is it fair to give them a poor grade? On the other hand, such students should not be led to consider themselves above average only to find later that they are deficient in academic ability. If a grade is necessary, a dual grading system might be used–one grade for effort and another for realistic ranking of functional ability. Such a system might prove useful not only for below-grade-level students but also for above-grade-level students who do only average work because of lack of effort.

What determines the difficulty of the color levels?

A Lexile® range has been assigned to each color level, with the Lexile® range increasing for each subsequent color. An official Lexile® score has been assigned to each reading passage. Then the reading passage has been placed in the appropriate color level based on the Lexile® score. In addition, the length of the reading selections increases at every level, and the comprehension checks and word study exercises become more mechanically complex and demand increasingly sophisticated kinds of thinking.

See the chart below for the reading level and Lexile® range for each color level in the 2b *SRA Reading Laboratory*.

COLOR LEVELS	APPROXIMATE READING LEVELS	LEXILE® RANGE
Lime	2.4	490L–540L
Green	2.6	540L–590L
Olive	2.8	590L–640L
Aqua	3.0	640L–690L
Blue	3.5	690L–740L
Purple	4.0	740L–790L
Violet	4.5	790L–840L
Rose	5.0	840L–890L
Red	5.5	890L–940L
Orange	6.0	940L–1020L
Gold	7.0	1020L–1100L
Brown	8.0	1100L–1150L

What about competition and cheating?

Competition and cheating are closely interrelated problems. If a student takes advantage of the ***Key Cards'*** availability to copy answers or if the student otherwise falsifies his or her scores, it is probably done in an effort to keep up with other class members or to get ahead of them.

For this reason, it is important in the initial stages of the program to convey the idea that multilevel work does not involve a race among classmates—that different students will be in different color levels because students differ, and this program provides materials that are appropriate for each one.

It is also important to minimize the idea that moving from one color level to another is the badge of success. This is *one kind* of success, which might be called vertical progress. But there is also horizontal progress—succeeding in each ***Power Builder*** a student works within a level, because each ***Power Builder*** presents new skills to master or different approaches to similar skills. Students should, therefore, be encouraged to see their goal as one of simply working as well as possible with the materials that are appropriate for them. They should not view climbing up the ladder of color levels as the only goal of their work. Obviously, you must play a key role in forming appropriate attitudes about what constitutes success.

Students hurt only themselves when they seek status among classmates by defeating the program's continuous placement mechanism and by moving ahead in the color sequence by means of copied answers or falsified scores. Those students miss needed practice and encounter material that is too difficult. You can try to communicate this idea, although obviously there will be resistance if a student has been taunted by a classmate for being "only in Orange," for example. You then face the traditional problem of how to motivate a student to do what's best in the long run when the student prefers to do what seems to provide immediate status and peer acceptance. It is a problem that occurs in all areas of student behavior when a competitive atmosphere exists, and it is by no means a unique problem to this program. Teachers who have found ways to remedy this problem in other areas of school life will probably handle it successfully in connection with this program.

If cheating is apparent, a confidential talk with the student is a good idea. You can stress the idea that "one only cheats oneself" and help the student understand that hurrying from level to level is not the aim of the program. Remember, too, that by spot-checking for errors and by praising accuracy and neatness in scoring, calculating, and charting, you can set up an atmosphere that discourages cheating.

Finally, remember that it is *not* cheating for students to look back at the story in order to answer the comprehension and vocabulary checks. Indeed, looking back should be encouraged as preferable to guessing or relying on uncertain recollections. Looking back is what we all do (and *should* do) in real-life reading situations when we want to be sure about what we have read. Once this is understood, some students may no longer have the need to misuse the ***Key Card*** or alter their scores.

What about record keeping?

Because *SRA Reading Laboratory* is student directed, you enter no scores and correct no papers. The student keeps all the necessary records on the Record Pages and the Progress Charts. The records each student maintains are invaluable guides to the diagnosis of his or her reading difficulties, progress, and long-range educational potential.

The value of these student-kept records is threefold:

(1) In parent conferences, the Progress Charts form an objective basis for interpreting school progress in the vital area of reading. They provide a direct and unbiased reflection of the student's day-to-day work.

(2) In student guidance, the Progress Charts represent a cumulative record of the student's actual *functional* ability to learn through reading. Such information is useful in helping both the parent and the teacher or guidance worker–as well as the student–in realistically planning the student's educational future.

(3) In curriculum improvement, analysis of the functional reading levels of pupils may indicate to the teacher or curriculum worker a need for revising upward or downward the difficulty level of offerings in the various subject areas. Such a study might point out a need for further steps toward individualizing learning opportunities.

APPENDIX B: Power Builder Titles

Level	Title	Word Count	LEXILE®
Lime	**Lexile® Range 490L–540L**		
1	*A Day at the Inside Beach*	286	540L
2	*Gwendolyn Brooks: Poet*	267	490L
3	*Deion's Coach*	342	490L
4	*Scientific Tools*	312	540L
5	*The Crow and the Pitcher*	393	500L
6	*The House Tigers*	355	520L
7	*Like Father, Like Daughter*	353	530L
8	*The Giant's Bridge*	401	530L
9	*Lights Out!*	347	530L
10	*Imani's Kwanzaa*	406	510L
11	*Find a Penny*	360	510L
12	*Natural Resources*	343	530L
Green	**Lexile® Range 540L–590L**		
1	*The House That Cleans Itself*	329	560L
2	*They Made It to the Top*	368	560L
3	*Life-Saving Hero*	364	580L
4	*The Mystery of the Monarchs*	397	540L
5	*How Fire Came to Earth*	325	570L
6	*How Does It Taste?*	424	560L
7	*Helen Keller*	363	590L
8	*Ski Hero*	442	550L
9	*Anna Sewell's Famous Horse*	460	560L
10	*Nature's Balance*	439	540L
11	*The Picture of the Fish*	331	540L
12	*Molly Pitcher*	468	570L

Level	Title	Word Count	LEXILE®
Olive	**Lexile® Range 590L–640L**		
1	*Time Travelers*	380	640L
2	*The Rooster's Escape*	438	630L
3	*Locks and Keys*	413	590L
4	*A Boy Becomes a King*	526	610L
5	*Otter Play*	527	600L
6	*Emily Dickinson*	427	610L
7	*The Case of the Missing Glasses*	481	590L
8	*Chinese New Year*	425	590L
9	*The Goose That Laid the Golden Eggs*	491	620L
10	*On the Right Track*	471	590L
11	*The Underwater Forest*	501	620L
12	*And Away We Go!*	458	600L
Aqua	**Lexile® Range 640L–690L**		
1	*Alice's Adventures*	494	650L
2	*What Do You Think I Am?*	515	640L
3	*Canine Police Officer*	529	690L
4	*A Clever Match*	482	690L
5	*The Shantyman*	561	640L
6	*Long-Distance Friendship*	421	650L
7	*Arion's Song*	502	690L
8	*Maria Mitchell: Astronomer*	489	690L
9	*All Kinds of Tongues*	549	640L
10	*The Missing Map*	475	680L
11	*The Boy Who Wouldn't Grow Up*	456	640L
12	*Plants That Catch Their Food*	554	660L

Appendix B

Level	Title	Word Count	LEXILE®
Blue	**Lexile® Range 690L–740L**		
1	*Grayson's Surprise*	464	690L
2	*The Fuss about the Ferret*	488	690L
3	*Hibernation*	432	690L
4	*A Friend of Nature*	510	690L
5	*Bats!*	544	700L
6	*A Better Idea*	492	690L
7	*Tricked by the Lights*	480	700L
8	*The History of the Movies*	567	740L
9	*Be Yourself, Barbara*	493	740L
10	*Snow Child*	510	700L
11	*Running Like the Wind*	479	720L
12	*Our Solar System*	544	740L
Purple	**Lexile® Range 740L–790L**		
1	*A Royal Confusion*	638	770L
2	*The Stone Carver*	672	750L
3	*Snow Leopards*	748	780L
4	*Waiting Out the Thunder*	674	740L
5	*Going Up*	666	790L
6	*Annie's Parade*	681	760L
7	*Socks*	640	740L
8	*Earth's Energy*	737	780L
9	*Our Changing Earth*	651	790L
10	*Camp Tekbegone*	687	740L
11	*The Tale of Keira*	728	760L
12	*A History of England*	649	780L

Level	Title	Word Count	LEXILE®
Violet	**Lexile® Range 790L–840L**		
1	*Reindeer Winter*	644	820L
2	*Arctic Giants*	724	810L
3	*The Camel Family*	742	810L
4	*The King's Elephant*	723	790L
5	*Braille: An Invention of Lasting Value*	681	840L
6	*Gift Exchange*	700	820L
7	*Stealing Smells*	732	800L
8	*The Activity of Sleeping*	752	840L
9	*Surviving the Sinking Titanic*	671	810L
10	*A Robinson Marooned*	719	810L
11	*Interesting Iceland*	735	840L
12	*Tornado!*	683	840L
Rose	**Lexile® Range 840L–890L**		
1	*The Teamwork of Geese*	694	850L
2	*The Disappearing Fish*	546	890L
3	*At Your Service*	574	890L
4	*Drones in Action*	685	880L
5	*The Notion of Motion*	791	870L
6	*The Accidental Pioneer*	849	850L
7	*Quick Thinking Saves the Day*	790	840L
8	*A Prince in Frog's Clothing*	823	880L
9	*Movie Effects and Computers*	747	880L
10	*Underwater Encounter*	833	840L
11	*King Midas*	909	850L
12	*How the Deer Got His Antlers*	939	840L

Level	Title	Word Count	LEXILE®
Red	**Lexile® Range 890L–940L**		
1	*Clinging to Hope*	906	910L
2	*The Fairy Tale Brothers*	846	920L
3	*Come to Puerto Rico!*	979	900L
4	*The Story of Swan Lake*	934	930L
5	*The Light Fantastic*	884	900L
6	*Your Marvelous Machine*	1060	930L
7	*Amazing Animal Navigation*	1021	920L
8	*Round the World with Nellie Bly*	919	930L
9	*Henry and Grammy*	940	890L
10	*Trapped in Tar*	879	940L
11	*More Than Meets the Eye*	985	920L
12	*The Sharing of Gifts*	823	910L
Orange	**Lexile® Range 940L–1020L**		
1	*The Longest Hike*	932	1010L
2	*The Saving Box*	1047	960L
3	*The History of Ice-Skating*	822	990L
4	*What Jim Hawkins Heard*	950	1010L
5	*Message in a Bottle*	1099	970L
6	*Ancient Egyptian Pastimes*	1011	1010L
7	*Katherine Dunham: Dancer*	1010	970L
8	*The Fantastic Mechanical Sea Monster*	1104	1020L
9	*The Hare and the Weathermaker*	1193	1010L
10	*Amateur Radio*	915	970L
11	*Bridges: Closing the Gap*	864	1020L
12	*Dramatic Realization*	1274	1000L

Level	Title	Word Count	LEXILE®
Gold	**Lexile® Range 1020L–1100L**		
1	*Running for a Cause*	1272	1020L
2	*To Sleep: Perchance to Dream*	1093	1070L
3	*The Witness*	1038	1050L
4	*Connecting Past and Present*	1114	1040L
5	*For the Love of Sharks*	1016	1100L
6	*A New Nation*	1120	1030L
7	*Dora's Project*	1259	1060L
8	*Earth's Energy Resources*	1058	1030L
9	*The Storm*	1046	1020L
10	*Mars 27*	1166	1030L
11	*Mixtures and Solutions*	1107	1030L
12	*Heat Transfer*	1096	1060L
Brown	**Lexile® Range 1100L–1150L**		
1	*Words on Paper*	1147	1110L
2	*Llama Patrol*	1093	1150L
3	*Tiny Nations*	1059	1140L
4	*Ebb and Flow*	1039	1110L
5	*Martha's Green Clean*	1141	1110L
6	*Plants and Animals*	1136	1120L
7	*An Unwelcome Visitor*	1197	1100L
8	*A Warm Song*	1130	1100L
9	*Water and the Weather*	1120	1140L
10	*The Grandeur That Was Rome*	1188	1150L
11	*A New Year's Celebration to Remember*	1061	1130L
12	*The Iliad and the Odyssey*	1146	1140L

APPENDIX C: Comprehension and Word-Study Skills Charts

Lime	Power Builder Number											
	1	2	3	4	5	6	7	8	9	10	11	12
Build Comprehension												
Author's Purpose												●
Cause/Effect									●			
Character			●		●		●	●		●	●	
Drawing Conclusions		●										
Main Idea				●		●						
Problem/Solution	●											
Learn about Words												
Vocabulary												
Word Meaning from Context	A	A	A	A	A	A	A	A	A	A	A	A
Using Words in New Context	B	B	B	B	B	B	B	B	B	B	B	B
Word Study												
Alphbetical Order		D		D			D		D			D
Blends	D					D					D	
Comparatives and Superlatives			E					E				
Compound Words					C					C		
Consonants	C					C					C	
Contractions				C					C			
Dictionary					E					E		
End Marks					D					D		
Index		E					E					E
Possessive Nouns			D					D				
Verbs			C					C				
Vowels	E	C				E	C				E	C
Word Classification				E					E			

Green	Power Builder Number											
	1	2	3	4	5	6	7	8	9	10	11	12
Build Comprehension												
Author's Purpose												
Cause/Effect					●		●		●	●		
Character		●						●			●	
Main Idea	●		●			●						●
Problem/Solution				●								
Learn about Words												
Vocabulary												
Word Meaning from Context	A	A	A	A	A	A	A	A	A	A	A	A
Using Words in New Context	B	B	B	B	B	B	B	B	B	B	B	B
Word Study												
Alliteration								E				
Alphabetical Order		D					E					F
Blends				C	C		C		C	C		C
Comparatives and Superlatives	E					D					D	
Compound Words			C									
Contractions		C		E					E			
Dictionary			E									
End Marks			D									
Internet						E					E	
Multiple-Meaning Words								D				
Nonfiction Books					E					E		
Possessive Nouns	D					C					C	
Verbs	C											
Vowels				D	D		D		D	D		D
Word Classification		E						C				

Olive	Power Builder Number											
	1	2	3	4	5	6	7	8	9	10	11	12
Build Comprehension												
Cause/Effect			●			●						
Character		●		●								
Drawing Conclusions	●											
Main Idea					●		●	●			●	●
Sequence									●	●		
Learn about Words												
Vocabulary												
Word Meaning from Context	A	A	A	A	A	A	A	A	A	A	A	A
Using Words in New Context	B	B	B	B	B	B	B	B	B	B	B	B
Word Study												
Alliteration	E					E						
Alphabetical Order					E							
Blends		C	C		C							
Comparatives and Superlatives				D					D			
Consonants								C, D				
Contractions		E										
Dictionary							E					E
Internet				E								
Maps									E			
Multiple-Meaning Words	D					D					E	
Nonfiction Books			E									
Nouns				C						C, D		
Question Markers											D	
Synonyms										E		
Verbs									C		C	
Vowels		D	D		D		C, D	E				C, D
Word Classification	C					C						

Aqua	Power Builder Number											
	1	2	3	4	5	6	7	8	9	10	11	12
Build Comprehension												
Cause/Effect			●							●		
Character	●			●			●				●	
Compare/Contrast									●			●
Drawing Conclusions					●							
Main Idea		●										
Sequence						●		●				
Learn about Words												
Vocabulary												
Word Meaning from Context	A	A	A	A	A	A	A	A	A	A	A	A
Using Words in New Context	B	B	B	B	B	B	B	B	B	B	B	B
Word Study												
Comparatives and Superlatives		D					D					
Dictionary					E						E	
Graphs										E		
Homographs				E					E			E
Letter Combinations											C	
Maps		E					E					
Nouns			C					C				C
Noun Markers			D					D				D
Question Markers				D					D			
Silent Letters										C		
Synonyms			E					E				
Two Sounds of *c*	C					C						
Two Sounds of *g*	D					D						
Verbs		C		C			C		C			
Vowels	E				C, D	E				D	D	

Blue	Power Builder Number											
	1	2	3	4	5	6	7	8	9	10	11	12
Build Comprehension												
Author's Purpose									●			
Cause/Effect			●				●					
Compare/Contrast												●
Fact and Opinion					●			●				
Main Idea		●										
Problem/Solution				●		●						
Sequence	●										●	
Setting										●		
Learn about Words												
Vocabulary												
Word Meaning from Context	A	A	A	A	A	A	A	A	A	A	A	A
Using Words in New Context	B	B	B	B	B	B	B	B	B	B	B	B
Word Study												
Dictionary				E					E			
Graphs			E					E				
Homographs					E					E		
Letter Combinations				C					C			
Nouns					C					C		
Noun Markers					D					D		
Question Markers	E					E					E	
Sentence Patterns	D					D					D	
Silent Letters			C					C				
Similes		D					D					D
Synonyms		C					C					C
Verbs	C					C					C	
Vowels			D	D				D	D			
Word Classification		E					E					E

Purple	Power Builder Number											
	1	2	3	4	5	6	7	8	9	10	11	12
Build Comprehension												
Cause/Effect			●									
Character		●					●			●		
Compare/Contrast	●							●				
Drawing Conclusions						●						
Main Idea					●				●			
Sequence				●							●	●
Learn about Words												
Vocabulary												
Word Meaning from Context	A	A	A	A	A	A	A	A	A	A	A	A
Using Words in New Context	B	B	B	B	B	B	B	B	B	B	B	B
Word Study												
Antonyms					D					D		
Internet		E					E					E
Irregular Verbs			E					E				
Jumbled Sentences				D					D			
Linking Verbs			D	C				D	C			
Prefixes	C, D					C, D					C, D	
Sentence Patterns				E					E			
Simple Sentences		D					D					D
Suffixes		C					C					C
Synonyms					C					C		
Tables	E					E					E	
Verbs			C					C				
Word Classification					E					E		

Violet	Power Builder Number											
	1	2	3	4	5	6	7	8	9	10	11	12
Build Comprehension												
Author's Purpose											●	
Cause/Effect					●							
Character				●		●	●					
Compare/Contrast		●										
Main Idea			●					●				
Sequence									●			
Setting	●									●		●
Learn about Words												
Vocabulary												
Word Meaning from Context	A	A	A	A	A	A	A	A	A	A	A	A
Word Relationships	B	B	B	B	B	B	B	B	B	B	B	B
Word Study												
Antonyms					C					C		
Graphs		E					E					E
Homophones			E					E				
Maps				E					E			
Metaphors					E					E		
Prefixes	C, D					C, D					C, D	
Prefixes in Context	E					E					E	
Sentence Patterns				C					C			
Similes					D					D		
Simple Sentences		D					D					D
Suffixes		C	C, D				C	C, D				C
Synonyms				D					D			

Rose	Power Builder Number											
	1	2	3	4	5	6	7	8	9	10	11	12
Build Comprehension												
Cause/Effect	●		●		●		●	●				
Drawing Conclusions											●	
Main Idea									●	●		
Problem/Solution		●		●								●
Setting						●						
Learn about Words												
Vocabulary												
Word Meaning from Context	A	A	A	A	A	A	A	A	A	A	A	A
Word Relationships	B	B	B	B	B	B	B	B	B	B	B	B
Word Study												
Adjectives						C					C	
Antonyms			C				D, E					D, E
Dictionary								E				
Homophones	E											
Latin Roots				E					E			
Maps		E										
Onomatopoeia						E					E	
Personification								C				
Prefixes				C, D					C, D			
Sentence Patterns		C										
Similes and Metaphors			D, E					D				
Suffixes	C, D				D	D				D	D	
Synonyms		D					C					C
Tables					E					E		
Verbs					C					C		

Red	Power Builder Number											
	1	2	3	4	5	6	7	8	9	10	11	12
Build Comprehension												
Author's Purpose							●					
Cause/Effect				●								
Character									●			●
Compare/Contrast					●						●	
Drawing Conclusions	●					●						
Main Idea		●								●		
Sequence								●				
Setting			●									
Learn about Words												
Vocabulary												
Word Meaning from Context	A	A	A	A	A	A	A	A	A	A	A	A
Word Relationships	B	B	B	B	B	B	B	B	B	B	B	B
Word Study												
Adjectives				C								
Antonyms					D, E						D	
Jumbled Sentences									E			
Latin Roots		E					E					E
Noun Phrases									D			
Onomatopoeia				E								
Personification	C					C						
Prefixes		C, D					C, D					C, D
Pronouns										C, D		
Reference Books	E					E				E		
Sensory Images											E	
Sentence Patterns									C			
Similes and Metaphors	D					D						
Suffixes			D	D				C, D				
Synonyms					C						C	
Tables			E					E				
Verb Phrases			C									

Orange	Power Builder Number											
	1	2	3	4	5	6	7	8	9	10	11	12
Build Comprehension												
Author's Purpose							●			●		
Cause/Effect								●				
Character				●					●			●
Compare/Contrast						●					●	
Main Idea		●										
Problem/Solution					●							
Sequence	●		●									
Learn about Words												
Vocabulary												
Word Meaning from Context	A	A	A	A	A	A	A	A	A	A	A	A
Word Relationships	B	B	B	B	B	B	B	B	B	B	B	B
Word Study												
Adverb/Adjective Markers											D	
Adverbs											C	
Antonyms				D					D			E
Graphs	E					E						
Homophones												D
Jumbled Sentences		E					E					
Latin Roots					E					D		C
Maps											E	
Noun Phrases		D					D					
Prefixes					C, D							
Pronouns			C, D					C, D				
Reference Books			E					E		E		
Sensory Images				E					E			
Sentence Patterns		C					C					
Suffixes	C, D					C, D				C		
Synonyms				C					C			

Gold	Power Builder Number											
	1	2	3	4	5	6	7	8	9	10	11	12
Build Comprehension												
Author's Purpose											●	
Cause/Effect						●						
Character			●						●			
Compare/Contrast								●				
Main Idea		●										●
Problem/Solution							●					
Sequence	●				●							
Setting				●						●		
Learn about Words												
Vocabulary												
Word Meaning from Context	A	A	A	A	A	A	A	A	A	A	A	A
Word Relationships	B	B	B	B	B	B	B	B	B	B	B	B
Word Study												
Adverb/Adjective Markers				D					D			
Adverbs				C					C			
Antonyms					E					E		
Dictionary			E					E				
Helping Verbs	D					D					D	
Homophones					D					D		
Latin Roots			D		C			D		C		
Maps				E					E			
Pronouns		C, D					C, D					C, D
Sentence Patterns	E					E					E	
Suffixes			C					C				
Synonyms		E					E					E
Verb Phrases	C					C					C	

Brown	Power Builder Number											
	1	2	3	4	5	6	7	8	9	10	11	12
Build Comprehension												
Cause/Effect				●					●			
Character					●						●	
Compare/Contrast			●			●						
Fact and Opinion	●											
Main Idea		●								●		●
Problem/Solution								●				
Setting							●					
Learn about Words												
Vocabulary												
Word Meaning from Context	A	A	A	A	A	A	A	A	A	A	A	A
Word Relationships	B	B	B	B	B	B	B	B	B	B	B	B
Word Study												
Antonyms					D					D		
Conjunctions				E				E			E	
Euphemisms					E					E		
Graphs	E		E			E			E			
Homophones		E					E					E
Latin Roots		D	D				D	D				D
Prefixes		C	C				C	C				C
Prepositional Phrases				C					C			
Prepositions				D					D			
Suffixes	C, D					C, D					C, D	
Synonyms					C					C		

Student Resources

The following section contains resources for your students. You will copy and distribute these materials as needed. These resources include:

- Home Connection Letter–As you begin ***SRA Reading Laboratory*** with your students, copy the home connection letter and distribute it to students to take home and share with their parents or guardians.
- Starting Level Guide–This will be used to determine the color level at which each student should enter the ***Power Builder*** component.
- Power Builder Starter Story–This will be used to acquaint students with the ***Power Builder*** procedures.
- Power Builder Record Page–Students write their answers to the ***Power Builder*** questions on these pages.
- Power Builder Progress Charts–These allow students and you to track their progress as they work through the ***Power Builders.***
- Rate Builder Record Page–Students write their answers to the ***Rate Builder*** questions on these pages.
- Rate Builder Progress Chart–Students chart their progress as they read through the ***Rate Builders.***
- Skill Builder Record Page–Students record their scores for ***Skill Builders.***
- Conversion Table–Students use this table to determine the percentage of their correct number of answers.

Ordering SRA Reading Laboratory® Student Record Books

In place of using the materials in the Student Resources section, keep students organized with their own individual books. Students can use their books to record answers to questions, correct their work, and record their scores and progress, promoting student accountability and ownership.

To order printed copies of the Student Record Book, visit: **https://www.mheducation.com/prek-12/explore/create-easy-order.** You can quickly find the appropriate level Student Record Book by searching for ISBN 9781309122051.

Home Connection Letter

This school year your child will be using the ***SRA Reading Laboratory*** program. This multileveled system of individualized instruction will provide your child with reading practice.

SRA Reading Laboratory offers high-interest fiction and nonfiction reading passages that cover a wide range of topics. The reading passages are divided into levels. Each level is represented by a different color, and each color is more difficult to read than the previous color.

Your child will move through the levels at his or her own pace, while working toward the following goals:

- To develop comprehension, vocabulary, word analysis, and study skills
- To reinforce specific skills to help your child become a proficient reader
- To interest your child in reading and to enlarge his or her specific knowledge, using a wide array of quality fiction and nonfiction selections
- To develop as an independent reader with strong comprehension skills, endurance, and confidence
- To develop the sense of personal responsibility by taking charge of his or her own learning

Millions of students have been using and enjoying ***SRA Reading Laboratory*** over the years. I'm sure your child will enjoy it too.

Throughout the year, engage with your child about what he or she is learning. Use the questions that follow as guides.

- Did you enjoy your latest reading passage? Explain why or why not.
- What new vocabulary or ideas did you learn?
- How are you progressing?
- How are these passages helping you improve your reading?

Starting Level Guide

Name_______________________________________ Date__________________

1. I can read as well as I would like to. ________ Yes ________ No (Check one.) If you checked *No*, complete all the statements below. If you checked *Yes*, skip 2 and 3, but complete 4, 5, and 6.

2. I would like to read better because I ____

____

3. I think the reasons I do not read as well as I would like to are ____________________

____

4. The kinds of things I like to read most are ____________________________________

____

5. The things I like to do in my spare time are ___________________________________

____

6. I have used ***SRA Reading Laboratory*** before. ________ Yes ________ No (Check one.) If you checked *Yes*, what grade were you in when you used it?

____

Here is a short story to read. After the story, you will find some questions. First, read the story, then read the questions and choose the *one best* answer to each question. Circle the letter of the best answer. While you are answering the questions, you may look back at the story.

Example

How far can a frog jump? A frog in Texas once jumped eighteen feet. He was in a frog-jumping contest. He became a world champion. They called him Sleepy Joe. He was nearly as big as a house cat.

1. Sleepy Joe jumped
   a. over a cat. **b.** eighteen feet. **c.** across Texas. **d.** around the world.

2. The frog was almost as big as
   a. a house. **b.** Texas **c.** a house cat. **d.** a tiger.

Story A

Bees talk to each other by dancing. Instead of words, they use dance steps. When a bee finds a good supply of nectar for making honey, it comes back to tell the other bees. It tells them by dancing.

If the nectar is close to the beehive, the bee dances in a circle. If it is farther away, the bee dances in a figure eight. The other bees know how far away the nectar is by the way the bee dances.

They know where the nectar is by the way the bee points when it wags its tail. The bee talks with its wings, too. They make buzzing sounds.

People have put dummy bees into hives to dance and make sounds like real bees. The real bees understood and flew to the sugar feeder that had been put out for them. By using these dummies, people have actually talked to bees.

1. Bees talk to each other by
   a. singing. **b.** dancing. **c.** flying.

2. Nectar is used for
   a. making honey. **b.** building beehives. **c.** dancing.

3. A dancing bee wags its tail when it
   a. dances in a circle. **b.** dances in a figure eight. **c.** points in the direction of the nectar.

4. People put dummy bees into hives to
   a. talk to the real bees. **b.** scare the real bees. **c.** play a joke.

5. The best name for this story would be
   a. Bees Make Honey. **b.** Bees Talk by Dancing. **c.** Buzzing Bees.

STOP HERE

Name______________________________________

Total correct, Story A ________

Total correct, Story B ________

Total score ________

Story B

Bionics—what is it? A new kind of airplane? A new kind of game? No . . . it's a fairly new science. The word is pronounced bī ä niks. Bionics began around 1950. In this science, humans learn from animals.

Animals have many unusual abilities we do not yet understand. How can birds fly thousands of miles across land and sea and return to their same feeding grounds each year? How can a bat fly in total darkness without striking the walls of a room? And—an even more puzzling question—how can it dodge the tiny wires scientists string across the room to study the remarkable radar system of this little "flying mouse"?

The sand flea, an insect no bigger than the head of a pin, navigates by using the moon's position. It does this with a light-sensitive cell and a microscopic, computerlike brain.

A dolphin can find a fish in a completely darkened pool. Does it smell the fish? We used to think so. But bionic scientists have found that this fishlike creature projects a series of sounds from its high, melonlike forehead. When these sounds strike an object and return to the dolphin—thousands of times a second—the dolphin can tell how far away the object is. Sound waves also tell the dolphin much about the kind of object it is. Dolphins have located objects a quarter of a mile away!

What does all this mean to us? By studying bats, dolphins, and other creatures, we have found valuable clues for designing radar and sonar equipment. These two are necessary for national defense. They have also become increasingly important in our everyday lives. Because of radar, our huge jetliners can fly in almost any weather. They can land on foggy airfields the pilot can't even see. Sonar helps fishers spot schools of fish deep in the ocean and bring better seafood to our tables. Humans have designed some wonderfully complex instruments and machines, but nature is still our greatest teacher. Bionics is helping us learn.

1. Bionics began
   a. more than a thousand years ago. **b.** about two hundred years ago.
   c. around 1950. **d.** around 1850.

2. The article says that we are studying animals in order to
   a. learn their names. **b.** make better pets of them.
   c. teach them to dodge wires. **d.** learn about their unusual abilities.

3. In this article, the bat has been called a
   a. flying mouse. **b.** radar system.
   c. wire dodger. **d.** computerlike brain.

4. The sand flea has a
   a. light-sensitive cell. **b.** computerlike brain.
   c. pinhead. **d.** Both **a** and **b.**

5. Dolphins are able to
   a. have melons in their foreheads. **b.** smell fish.
   b. send out sounds. **d.** Both **a** and **b.**

6. Dolphins can locate objects
   a. ten miles away.
   b. a quarter of a mile away.
   c. by smelling.
   d. several miles away.

7. Our radar and sonar equipment
   a. was developed by dolphins.
   b. was developed from the science of bionics.
   c. was developed by bats.
   d. is better than that of bats and dolphins.

8. Implied by not stated:
   a. Nature is still our greatest teacher.
   b. Sonar helps fishers spot schools of fish.
   c. Animals are good scientists.
   d. In some ways, animals are ahead of humans.

STOP HERE

Final Evaluation

Give your honest opinions on the questions below.

Name____________________________________ Date________________

1. Do you like the reading work you have been doing with *SRA Reading Laboratory?*
   ______ Yes ______ No (Check one.)

2. What have you learned from this work so far? ________________________

3. Has your reading work helped you in doing other schoolwork? If so, how? ____________

4. What did you like best about your work with *SRA Reading Laboratory?* ____________

5. What particular thing did you like least about this work? __________________

6. What suggestions can you give for making *SRA Reading Laboratory* even better? ____________

The Secret Culprit

1 Kia and Lucas ran across the beach. "We're here!" they shouted.

2 It had been a long time since they had visited Grandpa's house. They had forgotten how gigantic the ocean seemed and how much they loved the beach.

3 They picked a spot out of reach of the waves and built a castle in the sand.

4 The next day, when they ran to the beach, their castle was gone. The area was littered with shells and bushy seaweed.

5 "Someone smashed our castle!" Kia said.

6 "Don't be so sure," Grandpa responded with a smile. "There may be another culprit."

7 Kia and Lucas decided to investigate. They built another castle. Then they looked for signs of the culprit.

8 Late in the day, waves began to sneak up toward their castle. By dark, when the moon was out, the castle was flooded!

9 "The ocean swallowed it!" cried Lucas.

10 "Your culprit," Grandpa said, "is the tide."

11 Grandpa drew two circles in the sand. "These are Earth and the moon," he explained. "The moon causes Earth's tides. It has gravity that pulls Earth's oceans toward it. The bulge of water here is the high tide. In a few hours it will be low again."

12 "Because that spot will rotate away from the moon!" said Kia.

13 The next morning the tide was high again. They sat and watched as the waves drifted lower.

14 "Why are there high tides twice a day?" asked Lucas. "Earth only passes the moon *once* in our rotation."

15 "I'll explain why we get two high tides and two low tides each day," Grandpa said. Grandpa drew another bulge on Earth opposite the moon. "Here the moon's gravity is weaker," he said. "The water can flow farther from Earth. That creates another high tide."

16 "Ah," said Kia. "And here?" She pointed to another area.

17 "The pull of the moon and the water's force are about equal," said Grandpa, "so the tide is low."

18 Kia and Lucas spent the next week watching the tide. They noticed high tides bringing food for crabs on the beach. One day Lucas noticed something else. "Grandpa," he said, "the tide is higher today!"

19 "Indeed," said Grandpa, smiling. "Maybe the tide has another culprit helping it out." He pointed to the sky.

20 "The sun?" Kia asked.

21 "Correct," said Grandpa, drawing more circles in the sand. "The sun has gravity too, but we feel it less because it is so far away. When the sun and moon line up, the sun's extra pull makes a bigger tide. It's called a spring tide."

22 "What about when the sun is here?" Lucas asked as he drew a circle at right angles to the moon.

23 "It pulls against the moon's gravity," Grandpa said. "That makes weaker tides, called neap tides."

24 By the time Kia and Lucas went home, they had learned all about tides. They also remembered to build their sand castles high on the beach!

Build Comprehension

Write the letter of the best answer.

1. Why do Kia and Lucas shout at the beginning of the story?
   a. They step on a sharp seashell.
   b. The water is cold.
   c. They are excited to be visiting their grandpa.
2. At the beginning, what is the problem Kia and Lucas face?
   a. Their sandcastle is gone.
   b. They get sunburned.
   c. It is too rainy to play outside.
3. How do you think Kia and Lucas feel when they see that their sandcastle is gone?
   a. Afraid
   b. Happy
   c. Sad
4. How does their grandpa help them solve their problem?
   a. He helps them build another sandcastle.
   b. He explains high and low tides.
   c. He goes swimming with them.
5. Why does the sandcastle disappear?
   a. A high tide washes it away.
   b. Someone smashes it.
   c. Seaweed covers it.
6. When Kia and Lucas build another sandcastle, what will they probably do?
   a. Build a bigger sandcastle
   b. Build two sandcastles
   c. Build the sandcastle higher on the beach

Learn about Words

Vocabulary

A **You can often tell the meaning of a word by reading the words around it. Look at each number in parentheses. Find the paragraph in the story with the same number. Then find the word that fits the given meaning. Write the word.**

1. very big (2)
2. shaggy and thick (4)
3. cause; reason (6)
4. traces; marks (7)
5. swelling; lump (11)
6. spin; turn (12)
7. move; float (13)

B **A word may have more than one meaning. Its meaning depends on the way it is used. Look at each number in parentheses. Find the paragraph in the story with the same number. See how the word in bold type is used in the paragraph. Decide whether it has meaning a or b. Write *a* or *b*.**

8. **spot** (3)
   a. place; area
   b. to notice
9. **waves** (8)
   a. flaps; sways
   b. a moving swell on the water
10. **pull** (21)
    a. attraction
    b. to yank

Word Study

C **Some nouns end in *-ist* and *-ness*. Often *-ist* means "one who," and *-ness* means "state of being." Read each incomplete definition. Write the word that completes the definition.**

11. **motorist:** one who ______
12. **kindness:** state of being ______
13. **nearness:** state of being ______
14. **harpist:** one who plays the ______
15. **goodness:** state of being ______
16. **fairness:** state of being ______
17. **soloist:** one who sings or plays a ______
18. **fierceness:** state of being ______

D **The boat / swayed in the wind.**
(Subject) (Predicate)

Jazmin and Anne / played ball.
(Subject) (Predicate)

Each of the sentences above has a subject and a predicate. Read the sentences below. If the words in bold type are the subject, write *S*. If they are the predicate, write *P*.

19. Dustin **drove to the library.**
20. A bird **flew over our house.**
21. **The movie** was very scary.
22. This apple **is juicy.**
23. **Emma's cat** meowed.
24. Justin **is riding his bike.**
25. **Grandma and Grandpa** took us to the park.
26. Mateo **plays the trumpet.**

E **Some words are spelled alike and sound alike, but have different meanings. Such words have separate entries in the dictionary. For example:**

bill[1] account of money due
bill[2] mouth of a bird; beak
fly[1] insect that has two wings
fly[2] move through the air with wings
pupil[1] a student
pupil[2] the opening in the center of the iris of the eye

Read the sentences below and notice the words in bold type. Find the entry above that tells how the word is being used in each sentence. Write *1* or *2*.

27. Josh's **pupils** grew tiny in the bright light.
28. The **fly** landed on the lamp.
29. Each **pupil** was given a library book.
30. The duck grabbed the fish with its **bill.**
31. Did you **fly** in an airplane?
32. The waiter laid the **bill** on the table.
33. The parrot had a long **bill.**

Power Builder Record Page

Name ______________________ Date ____________

Power Builder Color ____________ Power Builder Number ____________

Starting time ____________ Finishing time ____________

Build Comprehension

1. ____ 2. ____ 3. ____ 4. ____ 5. ____

6. ____ 7. ____ 8. ____ 9. ____ 10. ____

Possible correct ____ Number correct ____ Percentage correct ____

Learn about Words

1. ____ 17. ____ 33. ____

2. ____ 18. ____ Possible correct ____

3. ____ 19. ____ Number correct ____

4. ____ 20. ____ Percentage correct ____

5. ____ 21. ____ **I believe my work on this Power Builder was**

6. ____ 22. ____

7. ____ 23. ____ poor ____ fair ____

8. ____ 24. ____ good ____ excellent ____

9. ____ 25. ____ **I can do better next time by**

10. ____ 26. ____

11. ____ 27. ____

12. ____ 28. ____

13. ____ 29. ____

14. ____ 30. ____

15. ____ 31. ____

16. ____ 32. ____

Power Builder Progress Chart

Name ____________________

Date													
Color													
Number													
Build Comprehension													
Percentage Correct	100												
	90												
	80												
	70												
	60												
	50												
	40												
	30												
	20												
	10												
	0												
Learn about Words													
Percentage Correct	100												
	90												
	80												
	70												
	60												
	50												
	40												
	30												
	20												
	10												
	0												

Rate Builder Record Page

Name ____________________

Date												
Rate Builder Color												
Rate Builder Number												
1.												
2.												
3.												
4.												
5.												
6.												
7.												
8.												
9.												
10.												
11.												
12.												
Possible Correct												
Number Correct												
Percentage Correct												

Rate Builder Progress Chart

Name ______________________________

Date													
Rate Builder Color													
Rate Builder Number													
Percentage Correct	100												
	90												
	80												
	70												
	60												
	50												
	40												
	30												
	20												
	10												
	0												

Skill Builder Record Page

Power Builder		Skill Builder			
Color	Number	Number	Title	Number Correct	Number of Questions

Conversion Table for Computing Percentage Correct from Number Correct

Possible Correct																		
5	Number correct	1	2	3	4	5												
	Percentage correct	20	40	60	80	100												
6	Number correct	1	2	3	4	5	6											
	Percentage correct	17	33	50	67	83	100											
7	Number correct	1	2	3	4	5	6	7										
	Percentage correct	14	29	43	57	72	86	100										
8	Number correct	1	2	3	4	5	6	7	8									
	Percentage correct	13	25	38	50	63	75	88	100									
9	Number correct	1	2	3	4	5	6	7	8	9								
	Percentage correct	11	22	33	44	56	67	78	89	100								
10	Number correct	1	2	3	4	5	6	7	8	9	10							
	Percentage correct	10	20	30	40	50	60	70	80	90	100							
33	Number correct	1	2	3	4	5	6	7	8	9	10	11	12	13	14	15	16	
	Percentage correct	3	6	9	12	15	18	21	24	27	30	33	36	39	42	45	48	
33 (con't)	Number correct	17	18	19	20	21	22	23	24	25	26	27	28	29	30	31	32	33
	Percentage correct	51	54	58	61	64	67	70	73	76	79	82	85	88	91	94	97	100

Key for Power Builder Starter

Build Comprehension

1. c
2. a
3. c
4. b
5. a
6. c

Vocabulary

A
1. gigantic
2. busy
3. culprit
4. signs
5. bulge
6. rotate
7. drifted

B
8. a
9. b
10. a

Word Study

C
11. motors
12. kind
13. near
14. harp
15. good
16. fair
17. solo
18. fierce

D
19. P
20. P
21. S
22. P
23. S
24. P
25. S
26. P

E
27. 2
28. 1
29. 1
30. 2
31. 2
32. 1
33. 2